The Greatest Woman: Every Man's Desire

Kayumba David

The Greatest Woman: Every Man's Desire

Kayumba David

Published by Kayumba David, 2024.

Copyright

THE GREATEST WOMAN: EVERY MAN'S DESIRE

First edition. December 9, 2024.

ISBN: 979-8230480075

Written by Kayumba David.

Also by Kayumba David

1

Grow a Backbone and Walk out of an Abusive Marriage

Standalone

Cry Africa The Western Guide on How Not to Fail the Continent
Grow a Backbone and Walk out of an Abusive Marriage
Hope and Healing: A Chaplain's Handbook
Visas: The Irony of Freedom
A Meeting with Majesty: The King's Call to Humanity
Visas: The Irony of Freedom
Love Beyond Time A Comedy of Divine Connection
Silent Complicity: State Sovereignty, Global Inaction, and the Rwandan Genocide
Bridging the Rift: A Pacifist Vision for the Israel-Palestine Future
Thanks to Calvary: A Salvific Treatise on the Cross
The centuries old swindlers
Harvesting Illusions: The Global Greed and the Pan-African Paradox
Hope and Recovery - A Chaplain's Handbook
The Only Crying God in all the Universe
LGBTQ Debunked by Natural Law
The Scandal of Gentleness: Who Was Jesus?
The Day of Reckoning: Leadership, Justice, and Divine Accountability

The Greatest Woman: Every Man’s Desire
The Lake of Truth
God's Interruptions

Watch for more at www.zcews.org.

Dedication

To the Black Woman,

You are the rhythm of the drums, the poetry in the winds, and the heartbeat of the earth. You are the quiet strength that rebuilds broken dreams, the loud voice that demands justice, and the light that illuminates the darkest paths.

This book is for you—the mothers who sacrifice so others may thrive, the daughters who dream of a better world, the sisters who hold communities together, and the warriors who fight battles seen and unseen. For every scar you've endured, every tear you've shed, and every triumph you've claimed, know this: you are not forgotten.

You are more than the cradle of life; you are the architects of resilience, the storytellers of culture, and the queens who wear their crowns with grace.

To the Black woman who has faced a world that sought to dim her light but has shone brighter with every challenge. To the woman who carries the legacy of ancestors and builds a future where her daughters will never have to question their worth.

This is for you—for your love, your courage, your laughter, and your spirit. You are not just the backbone of families and nations—you are the foundation upon which the world stands.

May these pages honor your story, celebrate your strength, and echo your voice.

With eternal gratitude,

Kayumba David

Preface

The story you are about to read is not just Africa's story—it is a testament to resilience, strength, and the indomitable spirit of a continent and its people. For centuries, Africa has been painted in shades of despair, often reduced to a backdrop of exploitation and tragedy. But this narrative is incomplete. This is the story of a woman who has bled but never broken, who has been betrayed but never defeated.

This book is not a lament—it is a roar. It is a reflection of history and a celebration of the present and the future. Through humor, sarcasm, and unflinching honesty, it confronts the suitors who sought to conquer Africa, the children who scattered across the globe, and the woman who refused to surrender her crown.

This is a story for those who believe in Africa's greatness and her ability to rise above the chains of history. It is a story that demands the world see Africa for what she truly is—a queen, a force, a beacon of hope.

To the reader: as you journey through these pages, I challenge you to rethink what you know about Africa. See her not as a bleeding woman but as the greatest woman she has always been.

With love, truth, and hope,

Keza HOPE

Introduction

The Enigma of the Greatest Woman

She was the kind of woman whose name, whispered, could launch ships and spark revolutions. The kind of woman you didn't just look at—you gazed, entranced, as though staring into the very essence of beauty itself. Her curves? Rolling hills that stretched as far as the eye could see, fertile and full of promise. Her sparkling eyes? Rivers that flowed endlessly, shimmering under the sun, teeming with life. And her skin? Rich, dark, and alluring, the kind of soil that birthed empires and nourished dreams.

Men wrote songs about her—epic ballads that celebrated her beauty, her generosity, her spirit. But they always left out the part where they tore her apart. You see, every man who laid eyes on her wanted her, but not for who she was. They wanted what she had.

She was mysterious, exotic, and infinitely desirable, but behind that enigmatic smile lay scars so deep they told a story of centuries—scars that crisscrossed her soul like the arbitrary borders drawn on her body by men who had never even seen her. They called it love, but it was always betrayal.

The world has known many great women, but none like her. She gave and gave, not because she was weak but because her spirit was unyielding. Yet, every man who claimed to love her left her bleeding. Some called her naive. Others called her resilient. But none called her equal.

A Beauty Coveted Across the Globe

It began with the first whispers. "Have you heard about her?" they said, leaning in as if the mere mention of her name was a secret worth stealing. "She's rich." But they weren't talking about money—they were talking about the treasures buried deep within her. Gold that glistened brighter than the sun. Diamonds so pure they could cut glass—and hearts. Her lands teemed with life, her forests stretched endlessly, and her rivers carried the promise of prosperity.

Her beauty was irresistible. Men crossed oceans for her, braving storms and certain death. And when they arrived, they fell to their knees, not in reverence but in greed.

Take the Portuguese, for instance. They were the first to dock at her shores, wide-eyed and hungry. They told her she was beautiful, that they admired her strength. But what did they do next? They built Elmina Castle in 1482—not as a palace for her, but as a fortress for themselves, a place to store the riches they plundered from her lands and, later, her children.

And the Dutch? Oh, they weren't far behind. They came bearing spices and promises, but they left with her dignity, turning Elmina into one of the largest slave-trading posts in the world. They didn't even have the decency to thank her for the free labor.

The First Scars

She thought the men would stop at her shores, but they ventured deeper. They weren't content with her gold, her ivory, or her spices. They wanted more—her people. And so began one of the darkest chapters of her life. Over 12 million of her children were torn from her embrace, shackled, and shipped across the Atlantic.

"They'll have a better life," they told her, smiling. But she knew better. Her rivers wept, her forests mourned, and her hills bore witness to the cries of the stolen.

The scars from the Transatlantic Slave Trade were deep, but they weren't the last. Her beauty was too intoxicating, her wealth too tempting.

The Men Who Promised to Stay

Then came the suitors who promised commitment. They didn't just want her treasures; they wanted her entirely. They brought flags, guns, and a Bible. "We'll civilize you," they said. She didn't know what they meant until she saw them carving her body into pieces.

The Berlin Conference of 1884–85 was the equivalent of a bachelor party where the groom didn't even show up. In a smoke-filled room in Europe, men she'd never met divided her into neat little parcels. The British took her arms, the French her legs, the Belgians her heart. By the time they were done, she didn't even recognize herself.

King Leopold II of Belgium was the worst. He didn't just take; he mutilated. In the Congo, he turned her into a factory for rubber, cutting off the hands of her children when they didn't work fast enough. Over 10 million lives lost, all in the name of profit. And yet, he had the audacity to call it philanthropy.

The Woman Who Gave Everything

They called her "Mother Africa," but they treated her like a mistress—loved in secret, exploited in the open. They built empires on her back, using her gold to mint coins, her diamonds to crown queens, her oil to fuel their industries. And when she cried out in pain, they told her to be grateful.

Even when they finally left, they didn't truly leave. They handed her keys to a house she no longer recognized, but they kept a spare set for themselves.

"They love me," she told herself, over and over, as they returned with new promises. Loans instead of chains. Investments instead of invasions. But it was always the same. Every man who claimed to love her left her worse off than before.

This is her story—the story of the greatest woman the world has ever known. A woman who gave everything, only to be plundered. But don't pity her. She is still standing. She is still fighting. And she is still beautiful.

Let me know if you'd like me to expand or add even more detailed historical references to this introduction.

1

The First Lover – Chains of Love

He wasn't the kind of man who knocked politely at the door or brought flowers to woo a lady. No, this one came with shackles hidden behind his back and a smile that said, "Trust me." His eyes gleamed as he looked at her, not with admiration, but with the cold calculation of a thief assessing how much he could carry. He didn't just see her beauty—her abundant lands, her strong, able children, her infinite resources. He saw a treasure trove waiting to be plundered.

"You're fertile," he said. She thought he was admiring her lush fields and endless greenery. Little did she know, he wasn't talking about her land.

He offered trinkets in exchange for her children. Bright beads, cheap cloth, and the occasional musket—all things shiny enough to distract from the gravity of what was happening. Africa, still innocent, still trusting, believed in the exchange. "What harm could come from giving away a few?" she thought. After all, this was just trade, wasn't it?

But the man was insatiable. One child turned into ten. Ten became hundreds. Hundreds became millions. Soon, her coasts were lined with ships that were not bringing gifts, but taking them. The sound of shackles clinking replaced the songs of her people, and the laughter of her children faded into the horizon as they were dragged into an abyss called the *Middle Passage.*

The Business of Betrayal

The first ports were built under the guise of partnership. Elmina Castle, for example, constructed by the Portuguese in 1482, was presented as a trading post. A simple place for goods to pass hands, they said. What they didn't mention was that those "goods" would soon include human beings.

The Dutch saw the potential for profit and took over Elmina in 1637, turning it into one of the largest slave-trading hubs in history. Thousands upon thousands of men, women, and children were crammed into its dark, airless dungeons, waiting for ships that would carry them across the Atlantic. Many didn't survive the wait.

The survivors were dragged onto ships like cattle and packed so tightly that they couldn't even sit up. Disease spread faster than the waves could carry them, and the ones who succumbed were simply tossed overboard. The ocean became a graveyard, the water itself mourning the loss of so many lives.

A Trade in Tears

The man told her this was for her own good. "They'll have a better life," he said, flashing that same deceitful smile. But she wasn't naive anymore. She could hear the cries of her children, even from across the seas.

The *Middle Passage* was a journey of unspeakable horror. Over 12 million Africans were forcibly taken from their homes, but only about 10 million made it to the Americas alive. They arrived stripped of their names, their languages, their cultures, and their dignity.

And yet, the man kept coming back for more. From Senegal to Angola, her coasts became known as the Slave Coast, the Gold Coast, the Ivory Coast—names that spoke not of her identity, but of her exploitation.

Humor Amid Tragedy

- "He promised her the world, but all she got was the sound of shackles clinking like a tragic melody."
- "She thought she'd be hosting trade fairs. Instead, she got farewells."

- "He said he loved her children. She didn't realize he meant as free labor."

The Weight of Loss

As the years turned into centuries, the man grew rich off her children's backs. Sugar plantations in the Caribbean, cotton fields in America, and tobacco farms in the South—all of it built on the blood, sweat, and tears of her stolen sons and daughters.

Africa, once vibrant and teeming with life, began to wither. Her villages were emptied, her families torn apart. The heartbeat of her land slowed as she realized that she hadn't just lost her children—she'd lost a piece of her soul.

Her rivers wept, her forests mourned, and her hills stood silent witnesses to the tragedy. She wondered if she could ever recover, if the scars left by this first lover would ever fade.

But even in her grief, she held on to hope. Her strength was vast, her spirit unbreakable. She would survive this, she told herself. She had to.

This chapter ends with Africa standing at the edge of her shores, watching the horizon where her children disappeared. She vows to endure, but the weight of betrayal is heavy, and she wonders how many more suitors will come bearing promises, only to leave her bleeding.

Would you like to explore deeper insights into specific historical events within this chapter or expand on its emotional resonance?

2

The Suitor with the Crown – Civilization and Chains

He arrived with grandeur, wearing a crown that sparkled in the sunlight and carrying a map so pristine you'd think it held the secrets to the universe. "I'll civilize you," he declared with a pompous grin, as though Africa hadn't birthed civilizations when his ancestors were still figuring out how to club each other for food. He spoke of progress, but what he brought was a map, a pen, and a hunger so insatiable that even her vast lands would not be enough.

"You're a wild land," he said, "untamed and chaotic. You need structure, order, borders." She thought he meant harmony, cooperation, and unity. But when he pulled out his map at the Berlin Conference of 1884–85, it became clear: he was less of a suitor and more of a butcher.

The Great Carve-Up

The Berlin Conference was a party to which Africa wasn't invited—an event where 14 European nations gathered around a table to decide her fate. They didn't care that she already had kingdoms, empires, and systems of governance. The Ashanti in Ghana, the Zulu in South Africa, the Kingdom of Kongo—none of it mattered to them. As far as they were concerned, she was a blank slate, a canvas for their ambitions.

With rulers in hand, they carved her up like a Sunday roast. Borders were drawn with no regard for her rivers, mountains, or, most importantly, her people. Tribes were split, families separated, and rivals were forced into artificial unions that would later ignite endless conflict. They called it progress. She called it partition.

- **Historical Reference:** The Berlin Conference (1884–85), where European powers divided Africa into colonies without African representation.

- **Key Players:** Britain, France, Germany, Belgium, Portugal, and others, each vying for the largest slice of the "African cake."

The Crown's Gifts: Civilization and Chains

He promised her civilization as though she were some lost, aimless child. "We'll bring you schools, roads, and hospitals," he said, but neglected to mention the cost: her freedom, her culture, her identity. He built railroads, yes—but only to carry her gold, diamonds, and rubber to the ports. He built schools, too—but only to teach her children to obey him. And the hospitals? Well, they were more for his soldiers than her people.

Take King Leopold II of Belgium, for instance. He didn't just want a piece of her; he wanted all of her heart. In the Congo Free State, his rule became one of the most brutal chapters in her history. Under the guise of bringing Christianity and civilization, Leopold turned the Congo into a rubber factory. Villages were burned, and those who didn't meet rubber quotas had their hands cut off. Over 10 million lives were lost, but Leopold still managed to smile for the cameras, calling himself a humanitarian.

And then there was Britain, the ever-pragmatic suitor. In East Africa, they built railways and cities, but only after stealing her land and turning her people into tenants on their own soil. The British Empire's dominance stretched across vast parts of Africa, including Kenya, South Africa, and Nigeria. But their rule wasn't without resistance—figures like Dedan Kimathi of the Mau Mau uprising and the Zulu King Cetshwayo showed that her spirit could not be entirely subdued.

- **Historical Reference:**
    - King Leopold II's atrocities in the Congo, resulting in the deaths of millions.
    - The British colonization of Kenya and the Mau Mau uprising.

- ◦ The Herero and Namaqua genocide in Namibia, where German colonizers systematically exterminated entire populations.

The Wrath of the Kaiser's Men

And let's not forget Germany, the "new kid" on the imperialist block. Eager to prove his might, Kaiser Wilhelm sent his troops to Namibia, where the Herero and Namaqua people dared to resist colonization. The result? Genocide. Over 80% of the Herero and Namaqua populations were wiped out, their lands stolen, and their people driven into the desert to die of thirst and starvation. This was the so-called gift of European civilization.

Humor Amid the Chains

- "He said, 'I bring civilization.' She thought he meant schools and roads, not whips and chains."
- "They had a party in Berlin to decide her fate. She didn't even get an invitation. Typical."
- "He brought her Christianity but forgot to mention he'd be taking her gold and her soul as a tithe."

Africa Divided, Africa Subdued

By the end of the 19th century, Africa was unrecognizable. Her once-unified kingdoms and empires were now patchworks of European colonies, each ruled by men who spoke different languages but shared the same appetite for exploitation. Her gold funded their wars. Her diamonds crowned their queens. Her rubber fueled their industries. And her pride? That was buried under the weight of their lies.

She looked at herself in the mirror, trying to recognize the woman she once was. Her body was covered in scars, her spirit battered. Was this her destiny? To be forever divided, forever subdued?

But even in the darkest corners of her heart, a flame still burned. It was faint, almost imperceptible, but it was there—a reminder that she had survived centuries of betrayal before and would survive this, too.

This chapter ends with Africa standing amidst the ruins of her divided lands, her gaze fixed on the horizon. She wonders how long this suitor with the crown will stay and how much more he'll take before he's done. But she knows one thing: she may be down, but she's not out.

3

The Generous Tyrant – Freedom with a Catch

He swept in with the theatrics of a Shakespearean actor, declaring with great fanfare, "I'm leaving! You're free now!" The crowd erupted into cheers, banners were raised, and hope filled the air. Africa thought, *Finally, my time has come. The tyrant is gone, and I can rebuild my house.*

But as the dust settled, she realized something was off. The doors were unlocked, yes, but the house still had surveillance cameras. The landlord had moved out, but he left his keys—and his friends—with the new tenants.

This was freedom, yes, but freedom with strings attached. The kind of freedom where you're allowed to breathe but not too deeply, speak but not too loudly, and own your land—but only as long as you're willing to lease it back to him at a discount.

The Illusion of Independence

The 1950s and 1960s were painted as Africa's golden era of liberation. One by one, nations broke free from their colonial rulers. Ghana, led by the fiery and visionary Kwame Nkrumah, was the first to declare independence in 1957. "We must prove that the Black man is capable of managing his own affairs," he proclaimed. Across the continent, similar declarations rang out as countries from Nigeria to Kenya to Algeria shed the colonial yoke.

But this freedom wasn't the fairy tale it seemed.

France's "Gracious Exit": France handed over flags and constitutions to its former colonies in West Africa but left behind the CFA Franc—a currency system that kept these nations tethered to French control. Fifty percent of their reserves remained in French banks, and any major economic decisions required approval from Paris. Independence, but with a "babysitter."

Belgium's Farewell Gift to Congo: Belgium's exit from Congo in 1960 was a masterclass in chaos. They gave Congo exactly six months to prepare for independence, leaving behind just **17 college graduates** in a country of over 14 million people. Patrice Lumumba, Congo's first Prime Minister, dared to dream of a truly independent Congo, one that would control its resources and chart its own destiny. But the West had other ideas. Within a year, Lumumba was assassinated, with Belgian and CIA operatives pulling the strings. Congo's destiny was handed to Mobutu Sese Seko, a dictator who plundered billions while his people starved.

Britain's Silent Strings: Britain, too, exited its colonies with a wink and a handshake, but not before ensuring its economic and political interests were protected. Kenya's independence came with scars, as the Mau Mau uprising had been brutally crushed, leaving thousands of Kikuyu people dead or in concentration camps. Yet, the British handed over power to elites who were willing to continue serving British interests.

Democracy or Charade?

The suitor taught her democracy—at least his version of it. Elections were introduced, but they were rigged before the first vote was cast. Leaders who aligned themselves with socialist or Pan-African ideals were swiftly removed.

Kwame Nkrumah: In Ghana, Nkrumah dreamed of a united Africa that could stand as an equal to the West. His socialist policies and bold rhetoric made him a target. In 1966, a coup orchestrated with CIA backing ousted him, leaving Ghana in political turmoil.

Thomas Sankara: Decades later, Thomas Sankara of Burkina Faso tried to rewrite the rules. He refused to play the suitor's game, rejecting foreign aid, prioritizing local industry, and empowering women. But his audacity was his downfall. In 1987, his closest ally, Blaise Compaoré, with French backing, assassinated him.

Lumumba's Assassination: Patrice Lumumba's fate remains the quintessential example of the suitor's invisible hand. His call for Congo's resources to benefit its people, rather than foreign corporations, sealed his fate. His murder not only robbed Congo of a leader but sent a chilling message to other African nations daring to dream of true independence.

Economies Built on Sand

Economic independence was another illusion. The suitor had designed Africa's economies during colonization to serve his needs, and he wasn't about to let that change.

Cash Crops Over Food Security: Colonies had been forced to grow cash crops—cocoa, cotton, tea—for export, rather than food for local consumption. After independence, this pattern continued, ensuring that Africa remained a supplier of raw materials while the suitor reaped the profits.

Debt as the New Chain: Loans became the suitor's new weapon of choice. Institutions like the IMF and World Bank offered money with strings so tight they strangled any chance of progress. Structural Adjustment Programs (SAPs) demanded that nations slash public spending, privatize industries, and open their markets to foreign companies.

Take Zambia, for example. Once rich with copper reserves, the country was forced to sell off its mines under SAPs. By the 1990s, Zambia was drowning in debt, with poverty rates soaring. "Tighten your belt," the suitor said, as though Zambia hadn't already been starving.

The Puppet Masters

The suitor didn't just leave Africa to her devices; he installed puppets to dance to his tune. Dictators like Mobutu Sese Seko in Congo, Idi Amin in Uganda, and Samuel Doe in Liberia were propped up with weapons and money as long as they served foreign interests.

Mobutu, for instance, ruled Congo (renamed Zaire under his regime) with an iron fist while amassing a personal fortune estimated at $5 billion. His loyalty to the West earned him their unwavering support, even as his people languished in poverty.

- **Key Events:**
    - The rise of Mobutu Sese Seko, backed by the U.S. and Belgium.
    - Idi Amin's brutal dictatorship in Uganda, initially supported by Britain.
    - Samuel Doe's reign in Liberia, backed by the U.S. as a Cold War ally.

Humor Amid the Illusion

- "He said, 'You're free!' but forgot to hand her the keys to her own house."
- "He called it independence, but kept showing up uninvited to make all the big decisions."
- "He taught her democracy by ensuring his favorite candidates always won."

Africa's Realization

Africa, once hopeful and eager to rebuild, began to see the suitor's game for what it was. Her borders, drawn by foreign hands, were ticking time bombs of conflict. Her economies, shaped by colonial exploitation, remained fragile and dependent. Her leaders, whether dictators or democrats, often answered to powers beyond her shores.

"Is this freedom?" she asked herself. "Or just another form of chains?"

But even as the weight of betrayal bore down on her, she began to see glimmers of hope. Resistance was building. Leaders were rising who spoke of Pan-Africanism, self-reliance, and unity. Perhaps independence wasn't an illusion—just a dream deferred.

This chapter ends with Africa standing at a crossroads, her heart heavy with the burden of faux freedom but her spirit unyielding. She knows the fight isn't over—it's only just begun.

4

The Charmer – Bretton Woods and the Debt Trap

He was the ultimate salesman, the kind of charmer who didn't need a sword to conquer—his tools were contracts, briefcases, and a silver tongue. "We're here to help," he'd say, flashing that disarming smile. But his help came wrapped in invisible chains, the kind that felt light at first, only to tighten as time went on. Africa, still reeling from the scars of colonization, wanted to believe him. After all, who wouldn't want to rebuild their home after years of plunder?

But as she would soon learn, this charmer wasn't offering a helping hand—he was extending a chokehold. His name was Bretton Woods, and his accomplices, the IMF and World Bank, were his henchmen.

The Birth of Bretton Woods: A Suitor's Backstory

The Bretton Woods Conference of 1944, held in New Hampshire, was a meeting of global powers to design a new economic order after World War II. The result? The creation of the International Monetary Fund (IMF) and the World Bank—institutions that were supposed to stabilize global economies and foster development.

Sounds noble, right? Except Africa wasn't at the table. Decisions were made by Western powers, who designed the rules to favor themselves. Africa, still under colonial rule at the time, was nothing more than a footnote. When independence came decades later, these institutions were ready to step in—not as saviors, but as debt dealers.

The Trap Is Set

By the 1970s, many African nations were borrowing heavily. Who could blame them? Roads, schools, and hospitals needed to be built. Civil wars and colonial neglect had left economies in shambles. The IMF and World Bank were more than happy to lend money, dangling promises of prosperity like bait.

But the loans came with *conditions*. Not the "repay when you can" kind of conditions, but the "here's how you'll run your country" variety.

- **Case Study: Ghana's False Prosperity:**
  In the early years of independence, Ghana borrowed heavily to fund ambitious projects like the Akosombo Dam. But when global commodity prices (particularly cocoa) plummeted, the country struggled to repay its loans. The IMF stepped in with Structural Adjustment Programs (SAPs) that forced Ghana to cut public spending, privatize state assets, and devalue its currency. The result? Economic chaos and a population left without basic services.

Structural Adjustment Programs: The Hidden Knife

SAPs were touted as the cure for Africa's economic woes. Instead, they became the dagger that cut into the continent's social fabric. These programs demanded:

- **Massive Public Spending Cuts:** Governments were forced to slash budgets for education, healthcare, and infrastructure.
- **Privatization of State-Owned Enterprises:** Vital industries and services were sold off to foreign corporations.
- **Currency Devaluation:** This made exports cheaper (benefiting foreign buyers) but caused inflation and increased the cost of imports, hurting local populations.
- **Open Markets:** African economies were flooded with cheap foreign goods, devastating local industries.

Case Study: Zambia's Copper Collapse

Zambia's copper mines were once the backbone of its economy. Under SAPs, the government was forced to privatize the mines. Foreign companies swooped in, extracting profits while local workers faced layoffs and reduced wages. By the 1990s, Zambia was drowning in debt and poverty, despite sitting on one of the richest copper reserves in the world.

The Illusion of the Commonwealth: A Family in Name Only

Meanwhile, Britain offered another illusion: the Commonwealth of Nations. "We're family now," they said, inviting former colonies to join this exclusive club. But the Commonwealth wasn't a partnership of equals—it was a way for Britain to maintain influence without the hassle of direct rule.

- **Trade Inequality:** Commonwealth nations were encouraged to trade within the group, but the terms always favored Britain. African nations exported raw materials while importing expensive finished goods.
- **Political Puppetry:** Britain quietly supported leaders who aligned with its interests, while marginalizing those who didn't. Zimbabwe's expulsion from the Commonwealth in 2003, following Mugabe's land reforms, highlighted the hypocrisy.

The Commonwealth was, in essence, a glorified PR campaign for Britain—a way to stay relevant while pretending to care.

The Useless United Nations

And then there was the United Nations, the supposed champion of global peace and development. Africa pinned its hopes on this institution, only to be met with disappointment.

- **Rwanda, 1994:** The UN sent peacekeepers to Rwanda, but when the genocide began, they stood by and watched as over 800,000 people were slaughtered in just 100 days. The UN's failure to intervene remains one of its darkest moments.

- **Congo's Endless Conflict:** The UN's mission in the Democratic Republic of Congo (MONUC) was plagued by scandals, inefficiency, and a complete inability to bring peace to one of Africa's most resource-rich yet war-torn nations.

The UN loved to talk about Africa in its grand speeches, but when action was needed, it was all sound and no substance.

Debt: The Invisible Chain

By the 1990s, Africa's debt crisis had reached catastrophic levels. The continent owed hundreds of billions of dollars to foreign creditors, with interest payments consuming more than 40% of government revenues in some countries.

- **Fact:** By 2000, Africa was paying $15 billion annually in debt servicing—more than it spent on healthcare and education combined.
- **Case Study: Mozambique:** After borrowing heavily to rebuild following its civil war, Mozambique found itself spending more on debt repayments than on rebuilding schools or roads.

The IMF and World Bank offered debt relief programs, but even these came with strings attached. Nations were forced to implement even more stringent reforms, perpetuating the cycle of dependency.

Humor Amid the Suffering

- "He said, 'We're family now,' but he forgot to share the inheritance."
- "She borrowed money to build a hospital. He sent her a bill for the bricks—and interest."
- "The UN came to help, but mostly they just stayed for the photo ops."
- "He called it a loan. She called it a life sentence."

Africa's Awakening: The Beginning of Resistance

By the late 1990s and early 2000s, Africa began to fight back. Movements like Jubilee 2000 called for debt cancellation, arguing that the loans were illegitimate—incurred under corrupt regimes and unfair terms. The campaign gained traction, leading to partial debt relief for some nations.

In 2005, the G8 summit announced the cancellation of $40 billion in debt for 18 African countries. It was a small step, but it showed that Africa's voice could no longer be ignored.

The Chapter Ends with Africa's Realization

As the dust settled, Africa began to see through the charmer's illusions. The Commonwealth was a club with no benefits. The UN was a stage for empty speeches. And the IMF and World Bank were puppeteers, pulling strings to keep her bound.

But Africa was learning. She began to question the systems designed to exploit her. She knew the road to true liberation would be long and fraught with challenges, but she also knew this: the suitors who claimed to love her would never set her free. Only she could do that.

He didn't work alone. This suitor wasn't just an outsider; he had inside help. He knew that if he wanted Africa's diamonds, oil, and gold, he needed allies—those willing to sell her soul for a seat at the table and a share of the loot. Enter the collaborators: a group of African leaders who became the robber's accomplices. They smiled in public, spoke of development and progress, but behind closed doors, they signed away her treasures in exchange for personal gain.

Africa soon realized that while her suitor had the contracts, her leaders held the pen.

The Politics of Plunder

African leaders, especially in the post-independence era, inherited countries rich in resources but impoverished by colonial exploitation. They had a golden opportunity to chart a new course, to rewrite the rules and put Africa first. But many chose a different path. They became gatekeepers for multinational corporations, allowing the looting to continue under the guise of partnership.

Mobutu Sese Seko (Congo): Perhaps the most infamous example, Mobutu ruled Zaire (now the Democratic Republic of Congo) with an iron fist while amassing a personal fortune of over $5 billion. Under his watch, Congo's vast mineral wealth was handed over to foreign corporations. He claimed to be the savior of Africa, but his lavish lifestyle, funded by kickbacks from mining companies, told a different story.

- Mobutu's infamous leopard-skin hat became a symbol of excess, as he hosted extravagant parties while his people starved.
- He once built a $100 million palace in the middle of the jungle, complete with imported marble, while his country descended into economic chaos.

Omar Bongo (Gabon): As one of the longest-serving African leaders, Bongo turned Gabon into his personal fiefdom. The country's oil wealth flowed into his bank accounts, while multinational corporations like Elf Aquitaine (a French oil giant) secured lucrative contracts.

- French companies rewarded Bongo's loyalty with extravagant bribes, while the majority of Gabon's citizens lived in poverty.

Angola's Dos Santos Family: Angola, rich in oil and diamonds, became a playground for corruption under José Eduardo dos Santos. His daughter, Isabel dos Santos, became

Africa's richest woman, thanks to shady deals with foreign companies. Meanwhile, Angola's slums grew, and the wealth never trickled down.

The Cost of Collaboration

These leaders, instead of challenging the suitor, joined him. They became the middlemen, ensuring that foreign corporations could exploit Africa's resources without resistance. In return, they were rewarded with offshore bank accounts, luxury mansions in Europe, and endless flows of champagne.

Oil Deals in Nigeria: Successive Nigerian leaders signed deals with oil giants like Shell, Chevron, and ExxonMobil that left the government with only a fraction of the revenue. Billions were siphoned off through corruption, while communities in the Niger Delta were left to deal with the environmental fallout.

- In 2004, a report revealed that $16 billion in oil revenue had disappeared under President Olusegun Obasanjo's administration.
- Despite producing over 2 million barrels of oil per day, Nigeria struggled to provide electricity and clean water to its citizens.

Mining in Guinea: In 2008, Guinea's military ruler, Captain Moussa Dadis Camara, sold mining rights for the Simandou iron ore deposit—one of the world's richest—to foreign companies in backdoor deals. His administration pocketed millions, while Guinea remained one of the poorest countries in the world.

The People's Betrayal

For Africa's citizens, the betrayal was personal. These leaders were supposed to be protectors, heirs to the legacy of freedom fighters like Patrice Lumumba and Thomas Sankara. Instead, they became accomplices in the plunder.

Ken Saro-Wiwa's Struggle: In Nigeria's Niger Delta, writer and activist Ken Saro-Wiwa led protests against Shell's environmental destruction and the government's complicity. His reward? A sham trial and execution in 1995, orchestrated by Nigeria's military regime with Shell's silent approval.

- Saro-Wiwa's final words: "I am a man of ideas, fully aware of my responsibilities. I will die for the cause."

Land Deals in Ethiopia: In the 2000s, Ethiopian leaders began leasing vast tracts of land to foreign investors for commercial farming. Communities were forcibly evicted, and forests were destroyed, all to grow crops for export.

Humor Amid the Chaos

- "He called it foreign investment. She called it a sale of her soul."
- "Her leaders promised progress but left her with pollution and postcards."
- "She gave him gold; he gave her leaders Swiss bank accounts."
- "They said they were building the nation. Turns out, they were building vacation homes in France."

Resistance and Rising Awareness

Despite the betrayal, Africa's people began to fight back. Grassroots movements, whistleblowers, and independent media started exposing the deals and holding leaders accountable.

- **Botswana's Success Story:** Unlike many of its neighbors, Botswana used its diamond wealth to fund education, healthcare, and infrastructure. This was largely due to transparent governance and the refusal to let foreign corporations dictate terms.
- **Ghana's Fight Against Corruption:** In recent years, Ghana has taken steps to renegotiate mining contracts, ensuring a greater share of profits stays within the country.

Environmental Activism

Across the continent, activists have risen to challenge corporate exploitation and government complicity.

- **Niger Delta Movements:** Groups like the Movement for the Emancipation of the Niger Delta (MEND) have demanded compensation for environmental destruction and greater control over oil revenues.
- **DRC's Cobalt Fight:** Advocacy groups are calling out tech companies for sourcing cobalt from mines that exploit child labor and destroy communities.

The Chapter Ends with a Warning and a Hope

Africa realizes that her greatest enemies aren't just the suitors who come from abroad—they are also the ones who live in her own house. The leaders who were supposed to protect her have sold her out, leaving her poorer and more vulnerable. But she also sees signs of change: citizens rising, movements growing, and a new generation of leaders demanding accountability.

The road ahead will not be easy, but Africa begins to believe that she can reclaim her resources—and her dignity—if she stands united against both external and internal robbers.

6

The Bleeding Woman Speaks

For centuries, she had been silent, watching as one suitor after another came and went. Each left her weaker, her treasures plundered, her heart heavier. They called her beautiful, exotic, and irresistible, but none stayed to truly love her. None saw her for who she was beneath the gold, the diamonds, the oil, and the forests. Now, for the first time, the bleeding woman speaks.

Her voice is raw, weary, yet unbroken. It carries the weight of centuries, of betrayals too many to count. It is a voice that demands to be heard.

The Monologue

"They call me beautiful," she begins, her voice trembling with anger and pain, "but all they see is what they can take. My gold, my children, my forests. Am I nothing but a treasure chest to them? A map dotted with riches to be mined, stripped, and sold?"

"They tell stories about me. They write songs and poems, paint pictures of my curves and rivers, my mountains and skies. But none of their stories are about my pain. They don't speak of the chains that bound my children, the blood spilled in my forests, the tears that have flowed longer than my rivers. No, they call it history—as though that makes it easier to bear."

Her voice grows louder, filled with indignation. "Do you know what it feels like to be desired, not for who you are, but for what you can give? To watch them dig into your heart, your soil, your soul, and leave you empty? They call me 'Mother Africa,' but what mother would be treated this way by her children? By her lovers? By the world?"

Lamenting Her Losses

She pauses, as though recounting her wounds. "They came for my gold first. From the mines of Ghana to the hills of South Africa, they tore it from my skin. It crowned their kings, funded their wars, built their empires. And when it was gone, they left my people in poverty, toiling in the very mines that made them rich."

"Then it was my children. Millions of them, torn from my embrace and shipped across the oceans. They called it the 'slave trade,' as though my sons and daughters were commodities to be bought and sold. They built their wealth on the backs of my stolen children, and when slavery ended, they told me to be grateful."

"And when I thought they could take no more, they came for my land. They divided me at the Berlin Conference, carving me up like a cake. They brought guns and flags, and with them, they brought their lies. They said they would civilize me, but their civilization came with whips and chains. My forests became timber for their ships. My rivers were dammed for their power. My people became strangers in their own homes."

She pauses again, her voice softening. "And now? Now they come with contracts and briefcases, calling themselves investors. They promise me progress, but their progress leaves me polluted and poor. They take my oil and diamonds, leaving behind nothing but poisoned rivers and broken dreams. They call it development. I call it betrayal."

The Turning Point

Her voice shifts, now filled with introspection. "But maybe I'm part of the problem. Maybe I have let them take too much. Maybe I have been too trusting, too forgiving. I opened my arms to them, believing their promises, only to find daggers in their hands. Did I do this to myself? Did I love too freely, give too generously?"

She looks inward, questioning not just the suitors but herself. "Why do I keep waiting for them to save me? Why do I keep hoping they'll change? Maybe it's time to stop looking to them for solutions. Maybe it's time to look within."

Her voice grows stronger, more resolute. "I am not just the bleeding woman. I am not just a victim. I am Africa—rich in culture, resilient in spirit, and powerful beyond measure. I have survived centuries of exploitation, and I am still here. That is my strength. That is my story."

Humor Amid the Pain

Even in her sorrow, the bleeding woman cannot resist a touch of sarcasm. "They call me the cradle of humanity. Isn't that ironic? I birthed the world, and yet they treat me like the unwanted child."

"They said I was uncivilized. So they built their empires on my back and then called me lazy. They said I was savage, but who were the ones cutting off hands in the Congo and torching villages in Namibia?"

"They said they were bringing democracy. Funny, because I never got a vote in the Berlin Conference, or in the IMF boardrooms, or in their elections. But sure, let's call it democracy."

A New Resolve

Her monologue ends with a sense of determination. "I am done waiting for them to change. I am done hoping they'll see me for who I am. I don't need their validation, their pity, or their promises. I need my children to stand with me, to rebuild me, to remind the world that I am more than a resource to be exploited. I am a continent of possibilities, of dreams, of unshakable hope."

She takes a deep breath, her voice steady. "They have taken so much, but they will not take my future. That belongs to me."

Key Moments Referenced

- **The Slave Trade:** Over 12 million Africans forcibly taken across the Atlantic, their lives and cultures erased.
- **The Berlin Conference (1884-85):** Africa divided without her consent, setting the stage for decades of exploitation.
- **King Leopold's Congo:** Over 10 million lives lost to one man's greed for rubber.
- **The Niger Delta:** Oil extraction by Shell, leaving the region polluted and its people impoverished.
- **The Cobalt Mines of Congo:** The exploitation of resources critical to modern technology, at the expense of child laborers and devastated communities.

The Chapter Ends with Hope

As the chapter concludes, the bleeding woman looks toward the horizon. Her voice is softer now, but resolute. "I may be bleeding, but I am not broken. I am healing, and when I rise, they will see that I am more than my scars. I am Africa, and my story is far from over."

7

The Technology Tycoon – Blood in the Circuit Boards

He wasn't like the others. This one didn't show up with guns, maps, or contracts. He came with shiny toys, gadgets that beeped and glowed, promising a modern world where everyone would be connected. "This is the future," he said, waving a smartphone as though it were the Holy Grail. Africa, ever hopeful, looked at the screens and thought, *Maybe this time, it's real. Maybe this time, I will finally reap the rewards of my riches.*

But this suitor had no intention of sharing the future with her. The cost of his dazzling innovations was buried deep in her soil, extracted by her children working in the shadows. Her cobalt, coltan, and rare earth minerals became the backbone of his technological empire. Yet, while he prospered, Africa remained impoverished, disconnected from the very progress she helped build.

The Minerals Beneath Her Feet

Africa's soil holds treasures that fuel the modern world. The Democratic Republic of Congo (DRC), in particular, is home to over 70% of the world's cobalt reserves. This precious mineral is essential for lithium-ion batteries, which power smartphones, laptops, and electric vehicles. Without Congo's cobalt, the tech industry as we know it would grind to a halt.

Then there's coltan (short for columbite-tantalite), another vital resource found in abundance in the DRC. Coltan is used to make capacitors for electronics, ensuring that our devices don't overheat. Add to this Africa's reserves of gold, copper, and rare earth minerals, and it's clear: the continent is the beating heart of global technology.

But while the world enjoys the fruits of these resources, Africa is left with the bill.

The Cost of Innovation

The tech tycoon didn't bother to hide the exploitation. He didn't have to. African governments, desperate for foreign investment, handed over mining rights for pennies. Corporations swooped in, extracting billions of dollars in minerals while leaving local communities in poverty.

Case Study: The Cobalt Mines of Congo

In the DRC, cobalt mining is a brutal industry. Thousands of men, women, and children work in hazardous conditions, digging for cobalt by hand in what are called "artisanal mines." The term may sound quaint, but the reality is anything but. Workers toil in unregulated mines, often without protective gear, earning just a few dollars a day.

- **Child Labor:** UNICEF estimates that 40,000 children work in cobalt mines in the DRC. These children, some as young as seven, risk their lives daily, inhaling toxic dust and working in unstable tunnels.
- **Environmental Devastation:** Mining operations leave behind poisoned rivers and barren landscapes. Villages are displaced, and ecosystems are destroyed, all to fuel the tech tycoon's empire.

The Disconnect: Despite sitting on trillions of dollars' worth of minerals, the DRC remains one of the poorest countries in the world. Over 70% of its population lives on less than $2 a day. Meanwhile, corporations like Tesla, Apple, and Samsung rake in billions.

The Broken Promises of Progress

The suitor promised development, jobs, and prosperity. What Africa got was exploitation and dependency.

- **The Monopoly Game:** Multinational corporations dominate Africa's mining industry. Glencore, for example, controls several cobalt mines in the DRC, reaping enormous profits while paying minimal taxes.
- **Trade Imbalances:** African countries export raw minerals at low prices, only to import finished electronics at exorbitant rates. The value-added process—where the real money is made—takes place in factories in Asia, Europe, or North America, leaving Africa at the bottom of the value chain.
- **Electric Cars, Silent Costs:** As the world transitions to electric vehicles, demand for cobalt has skyrocketed. Yet, the communities extracting this critical resource see no benefits. Electric cars may reduce carbon emissions, but their production leaves a human and environmental toll in Africa.

Humor Amid the Tragedy

Even in her suffering, Africa can't help but laugh at the absurdity of it all.

- "He said his phone was smart. She wondered why it couldn't figure out how to give her a fair price."
- "She gave him the minerals for the gadgets he used to text other women."
- "He called it the future. She called it theft."
- "They promised connectivity. Turns out, the only thing connected was their bank accounts."

The Tech Tycoon's Web of Exploitation

The tycoon didn't just rely on corporations; he had help from governments and international institutions.

- **Weak Regulations:** Many African governments, under pressure to attract foreign investment, implemented lax mining regulations. Companies faced minimal oversight, allowing them to exploit both workers and the environment.
- **Tax Evasion:** Corporations used loopholes and offshore accounts to avoid

paying taxes, depriving African nations of billions in revenue.

- In 2020, a report revealed that the DRC lost $1.3 billion in mining revenue over three years due to corruption and mismanagement.

The Activists Fighting Back

Despite the odds, Africa's people are resisting. Activists, NGOs, and local communities are fighting to reclaim control of their resources.

- **Congo's Child Labor Lawsuits:** In 2019, human rights groups filed lawsuits against tech giants like Apple, Google, and Tesla, accusing them of profiting from child labor in cobalt mines.
- **Resource Nationalism:** Countries like Tanzania and Zambia have begun renegotiating mining contracts, demanding a fairer share of the profits.
- **Grassroots Movements:** In mining regions across Africa, communities are organizing to demand environmental protection and better working conditions.

The Ironic Disconnect

Africa's resources fuel the world's progress, yet the continent itself remains in the shadows. The irony is almost too much to bear.

- The DRC provides the cobalt for electric cars, yet its roads are unpaved.
- Africa supplies the gold for luxury smartphones, yet its schools lack electricity.
- The continent powers global connectivity, yet its own internet penetration remains the lowest in the world.

The Chapter Ends with a Realization

As Africa reflects on her relationship with the tech tycoon, she begins to see the pattern. He, like all the others, came not to uplift her, but to use her. Yet, she also sees a glimmer of hope.

"If I can control my resources," she thinks, "if I can break free from their grasp, then I can build my own future. A future where my children don't dig in the mines but design the devices. A future where the wealth beneath my soil stays in my hands."

8

The Unfaithful Suitor – The West and the East

He came bearing a red flag adorned with golden stars, draped in promises that glittered like the diamonds beneath her soil. "I'm not like the others," he said, his voice soft yet confident, a subtle jab at her past suitors. "I understand you."

At first, his offers were dazzling. Roads that stretched for miles, railways that whispered of progress, ports that promised to open her shores to prosperity. He didn't scold her about democracy or wag his finger at her leaders. He seemed to offer respect. "This is win-win cooperation," he said. *Finally,* she thought, *someone who gets me.*

But as the ink dried on the contracts—long and written in a language she didn't understand—she began to notice something familiar. The gifts came with bills she couldn't afford to pay. The promises of partnership felt one-sided. And when she looked into his eyes, she saw the same hunger she'd seen in the West's, the same desire for what lay beneath her soil.

The New Suitor: China's Rise in Africa

The rise of China as a global superpower reshaped Africa's landscape. While the West spent decades lecturing her about governance and democracy, China offered an alternative. "No strings attached," they said, "just business."

- **China's Belt and Road Initiative (BRI):** Launched in 2013, the BRI was a global infrastructure project aimed at connecting Asia, Africa, and Europe. Africa became a key focus, with billions of dollars invested in roads, railways, ports, and power plants.
  - **Case Study: Ethiopia's Railways**: China funded the $4 billion

Addis Ababa-Djibouti railway, a vital trade link. But Ethiopia now struggles with loan repayments, and the project's profits fall far short of expectations.

  - **Kenya's SGR Railway**: The $3.2 billion Standard Gauge Railway, connecting Mombasa to Nairobi, was touted as a game-changer. Instead, it operates at a loss, and fears linger that Kenya's port in Mombasa could be seized if the country defaults on its loans.

China's investments were undeniably transformative, but they weren't charity. Loans came with interest, and when countries couldn't repay, they risked losing control of key infrastructure.

The Jealous Exes: The West Watches Nervously

For decades, the West enjoyed unchallenged dominance in Africa. They built the rules, controlled the aid, and dictated the terms. But now, they were being sidelined. China's growing influence sparked anxiety in Washington, Brussels, and London.

- **The U.S. Response:**

-
  - The Trump administration unveiled the **Prosper Africa** initiative in 2018, promising to "unlock opportunities" for African nations. But the timing made it clear: this was less about helping Africa and more about countering China's influence.
  - U.S. Secretary of State Mike Pompeo warned African nations about China's "debt traps," while conveniently ignoring the West's own history of exploitative loans.

- **The EU's Pushback:**

-
    - Europe, not to be outdone, launched its **Global Gateway** initiative in 2021, pledging €300 billion for global infrastructure, much of it targeting Africa. It sounded promising, but African leaders couldn't help but wonder: where was this enthusiasm before China arrived?

The West, desperate to reclaim Africa's affection, suddenly seemed interested in her needs. But Africa had seen this playbook before.

"They both fight for my attention," she mused, "but neither cares for my heart. They only want what lies beneath my soil."

Promises Wrapped in Debt

China's approach was seductive, offering shiny infrastructure projects that the West had long neglected. But the fine print revealed the true cost.

-

Djibouti's Debt Spiral:

-
    - China built a sprawling port and railway in Djibouti, making it a strategic hub. But with debt soaring to over 70% of GDP, Djibouti risks losing control of its assets.
    - The U.S., with its military base in Djibouti, watched nervously, fearing that China's growing presence could disrupt Western influence in the region.

-

Zambia's Debt Trap:

-
    - Zambia borrowed heavily from China to fund infrastructure, but when copper prices fell, the country struggled to repay. In 2019, Zambia was forced to hand over control of its national electricity

company to a Chinese firm.

- **Sri Lanka's Warning:**
  - Although outside Africa, Sri Lanka's experience with China sent shockwaves across the continent. In 2017, Sri Lanka handed over control of its Hambantota Port on a 99-year lease after failing to repay Chinese loans. African leaders began to wonder: could this happen to us?

The Battle for Resources

The tug-of-war wasn't just about infrastructure. Africa's resources—oil, minerals, and rare earths—became the ultimate prize.

- **Angola's Oil Deals:**
  - China became Angola's largest trading partner, funding infrastructure in exchange for oil. But as oil prices plummeted, Angola struggled under the weight of its debt.
  - Meanwhile, Western oil giants like ExxonMobil and BP continued to exploit Angola's resources, ensuring the West still had a foothold.
- **Rare Earths and the Tech Industry:**
  - Both China and the West are vying for control of Africa's rare earth minerals, critical for smartphones, electric vehicles, and renewable energy. The DRC, with its vast cobalt reserves, finds itself at the center of this resource tug-of-war.

The Illusion of Partnership

Both suitors claimed to be partners, but their actions spoke louder than their words.

- **China's "No Strings Attached" Myth:** Chinese loans often required African governments to award contracts to Chinese companies, which used Chinese labor and materials. Local economies saw little benefit.
- **The West's "Aid for Influence" Strategy:** Western aid came with political strings, demanding democratic reforms or allegiance to Western agendas.

Africa, caught between these two powers, began to see the pattern. "They come with different flags," she said, "but their intentions are the same. They see my resources, my potential, my beauty, but not my worth."

Humor Amid the Chaos

- "He said he wasn't like my ex, but I caught him eyeing the same diamonds."
- "They both promised me progress, but I ended up with the bill."
- "The West said, 'Don't trust him.' I replied, 'You mean like I trusted you?'"
- "He called it win-win cooperation. Turns out, the only winner was him."

Africa's Awakening

Despite the challenges, Africa began to push back. Leaders, activists, and citizens demanded a new approach—one that prioritized African interests.

- **Tanzania's Bold Moves:** Under President John Magufuli, Tanzania renegotiated mining contracts and introduced policies that increased the government's share of mining profits.
- **The Africa Continental Free Trade Area (AfCFTA):** Launched in 2021,

the AfCFTA aims to boost intra-African trade and reduce dependency on external powers.

- **Grassroots Resistance:** From protests against exploitative land deals in Ethiopia to movements for resource nationalism in Zambia, Africans are reclaiming their agency.

The Chapter Ends with a Realization

As Africa reflects on her suitors, she begins to see the truth. "They come dressed differently," she says, "but they are all the same. They take, they leave, and they expect me to be grateful."

But this time, she's done waiting for rescue. "If I want to rise, I must rise for myself. If I want to prosper, I must chart my own path. They can fight over me, but my future belongs to me."

Would you like me to explore more specific case studies, such as African nations successfully resisting debt traps, or dive deeper into the environmental and social costs of these relationships?

9

The Puppet Masters – Dictators and Chaos

This time, the suitor didn't even bother to show up. Why would he? He'd perfected the art of remote control. Instead, he sent proxies—men with iron fists, overflowing egos, and a knack for enriching themselves while their people starved. These weren't lovers; they were tyrants, strategically placed to keep Africa bleeding while ensuring the suitor's interests were protected.

The real masters, of course, were far away, comfortably seated in Washington, Paris, London, and Moscow. They pulled the strings, made the deals, and orchestrated the chaos. They called it geopolitics; Africa called it betrayal.

Museveni: The Modern Puppet King

Among the pantheon of Africa's enduring strongmen, Yoweri Museveni of Uganda has perfected the art of playing puppet while pretending to be master of his own fate.

- **The Rise to Power:** Museveni came to power in 1986, positioning himself as a liberator who would restore Uganda after the horrors of Idi Amin and Milton Obote. The West applauded, hailing him as part of Africa's "new generation of leaders."
- **The Puppet Playbook:** Museveni mastered the game of pleasing his foreign backers while consolidating power at home. His partnership with the U.S. and Europe, under the guise of fighting terrorism and promoting regional stability, ensured a steady flow of aid and weapons. Uganda became a key U.S. ally, contributing troops to fight Al-Shabaab in Somalia and receiving billions in military support in return.

Behind the Curtain: While Museveni charmed the West, his regime systematically dismantled democracy. He clung to power through constitutional amendments, rigged elections, and brutal crackdowns on dissent. The 2021 presidential election, in which Museveni faced off against Bobi Wine, was marred by violence, media blackouts, and allegations of fraud.

- **A Personal Fiefdom:** Museveni's family dominates Uganda's government. His wife is the Minister of Education, his son heads a military unit, and his inner circle controls vast economic resources. While ordinary Ugandans struggle, Museveni's family enjoys the spoils of power.

Mobutu Sese Seko: The Blueprint for Lootocracy

Before Museveni perfected the art of puppetry, Mobutu Sese Seko set the standard. Installed by the CIA after the assassination of Patrice

Lumumba, Mobutu turned Zaire (now the Democratic Republic of Congo) into his personal ATM.

- **A Kleptocrat's Dream:** Mobutu's regime was the epitome of greed. He pocketed an estimated $5 billion while his country's infrastructure crumbled. His lavish lifestyle included a $100 million jungle palace and shopping trips to Paris on Concorde jets.
- **The Cold War Pawn:** The U.S. backed Mobutu as a bulwark against communism, ignoring his corruption and human rights abuses. As long as he kept the Soviets out, his reign of terror was tolerated.

France's Puppets: Françafrique

France had its own version of puppetry, known as *Françafrique*. This policy ensured that former French colonies in Africa remained economically dependent and politically loyal to Paris.

- **Omar Bongo (Gabon):** France's poster child, Bongo ruled Gabon for 42 years, enriching himself while French companies controlled the country's oil. In return, Bongo funneled millions into French political campaigns, ensuring mutual loyalty.
- **Jean-Bédel Bokassa (Central African Republic):** Bokassa declared himself Emperor of the Central African Republic in 1977, staging a coronation that cost $20 million—all paid for by France. When he became a liability, France orchestrated his removal.

Cold War Chaos: Proxy Wars and Puppets

The Cold War turned Africa into a chessboard. The U.S. and USSR supported rival factions, fueling endless conflicts to gain strategic control.

- **Angola's Civil War:**

    - The U.S. backed the anti-communist UNITA rebels, while the USSR and Cuba supported the MPLA government. The war, funded by foreign powers, killed over 500,000 people and devastated Angola's infrastructure.
- **Ethiopia's Bloody Alliance:**
    - Mengistu Haile Mariam's Marxist regime in Ethiopia, backed by the USSR, unleashed terror through its "Red Terror" campaign. Meanwhile, the U.S. supported Somali dictator Siad Barre, who invaded Ethiopia in 1977, sparking the Ogaden War.

The Economic Puppets

It wasn't just political puppetry—Africa's economies were also tied to foreign strings.

- **Structural Adjustment Programs:** The IMF and World Bank imposed harsh austerity measures, forcing African governments to cut public spending, privatize industries, and open their markets to foreign investors. The result? Widespread poverty and weakened institutions.
- **Resource Exploitation:** Foreign companies, often with the backing of corrupt leaders, extracted Africa's wealth while paying minimal taxes. In Nigeria, oil giants like Shell enriched themselves while leaving the Niger Delta polluted and impoverished.

Humor Amid the Horror

- "He gave her a husband who spent all her money on guns and gold-plated toilets."
- "They called it leadership. She called it looting."
- "He said, 'I'll protect you.' She realized he meant from her own people."
- "They fought communism with capitalism and left me with corruption."

Resistance and the Fight for Sovereignty

Despite the grip of puppet masters, Africa has always resisted. Movements for democracy and justice have risen across the continent.

- **South Africa's Anti-Apartheid Struggle:** The U.S. and UK supported apartheid South Africa economically and militarily, yet internal resistance and global solidarity forced the regime's collapse.
- **Liberia's Grassroots Revolution:** Women like Leymah Gbowee led peace movements that ended Charles Taylor's reign, showing the power of collective action.
- **Protests in Uganda:** Bobi Wine's rise as a political challenger to Museveni has galvanized a generation of young Ugandans demanding change, despite violent crackdowns.

The Cost of Puppetry

The legacy of puppet regimes is clear:

- **Weakened Institutions:** Leaders focused on enriching themselves rather than building strong systems of governance.
- **Resource Dependency:** Economies reliant on resource extraction, with profits flowing to foreign corporations.
- **Divided Societies:** Ethnic and political divisions exacerbated by foreign meddling and puppet rulers.

Africa's Awakening

The strings are beginning to fray. Across the continent, a new generation of leaders and activists is rejecting the era of puppetry.

- **Rwanda's Post-Genocide Model:** After the 1994 genocide, Rwanda rejected foreign interference, prioritizing development and stability under

President Paul Kagame.

- **Pan-African Movements:** The African Union and regional organizations are pushing for greater unity, seeking to end the era of foreign manipulation.
- **Citizen-Led Change:** From Sudan's revolution to Nigeria's #EndSARS movement, ordinary Africans are demanding accountability and transparency.

The Chapter Ends with a Question

As Africa reflects on the era of puppet masters, she asks herself: "How long will I allow others to pull the strings? How long will I accept leaders who serve anyone but me?"

She knows the fight isn't over, but this time, she's ready. The puppet masters may have written the script, but Africa is determined to rewrite the ending.

10

The Bleeding Woman Speaks

It was a moment centuries in the making. After enduring endless exploitation, betrayal, and pain, the bleeding woman finally stood tall and unleashed her voice—a voice heavy with sorrow, anger, and defiance. She wasn't asking for pity. She wasn't begging for help. She was demanding answers, accountability, and justice.

For too long, they had silenced her with contracts, coups, and the cold indifference of their progress. But now, she would be silent no more.

The Monologue

"You stole my children, my land, my treasures. You divided my home, planted seeds of hate, and watched me burn. When will it be enough?" Her voice trembles with rage, carrying centuries of unspoken pain.

"They call me the cradle of humanity. Is this how they treat their mother? They tore my children from my arms, shackled them, and shipped them across the seas. Twelve million stolen—packed into ships like cargo, their lives measured in profits. You called it commerce. I called it carnage."

Her eyes darken as she recounts her scars. "Then you came for my land. At the Berlin Conference, you carved me up like a cake, slicing through my rivers, mountains, and tribes with rulers and pens. You didn't even invite me to the table. My children were turned into strangers, forced to fight wars that weren't theirs, for flags they didn't choose."

"And when I dared to resist, you called me savage. When I fought for freedom, you called me dangerous. You murdered my visionaries—Patrice Lumumba, Thomas Sankara, Steve Biko—because they dreamed of an Africa that didn't bow to you."

She takes a deep breath, her voice growing steadier. "You said you'd bring civilization. Is this what civilization looks like? Rubber quotas in the Congo, with hands chopped off as punishment. Apartheid in South Africa, where my children lived as outcasts in their own land. Oil spills in the Niger Delta, choking my rivers and poisoning my soil. If this is civilization, you can keep it."

Calling Out the Suitors by Name

She names them all—every suitor who came promising love but left her bleeding.

- **The Slave Traders:** "Portugal, Britain, Spain, France, Holland—your ships carried away my sons and daughters, stripping my villages bare. You built your empires on their backs, yet you speak of human rights and liberty. Where was that liberty when my children were sold on auction blocks?"

  The Colonizers: "You didn't just take my gold, my diamonds, my oil—you took my dignity. Belgium, King Leopold called himself a humanitarian as he slaughtered ten million of my children in the Congo. France, you gave me *Françafrique*, a leash disguised as a partnership. Britain, your Union Jack waved over stolen lands and broken families. How dare you speak of justice while holding the keys to my stolen treasures in your museums?"

  The Neocolonialists: "You left, but you never really left. The IMF, the World Bank, the WTO—you chained me with debt instead of shackles. You told me to privatize my water, my schools, my hospitals. You took my sovereignty and called it structural adjustment. You took my resources and called it globalization."

The New Suitors: "China, you came with roads and railways, but your loans are just another set of chains. You said you weren't like the West, but I caught you eyeing the same diamonds. And to the West—you stand there accusing China of exploiting me as if you didn't write the playbook. You're all the same. You see my wealth, but never my worth."

A Reflection on Pain and Resilience

"They say I am poor, but how can that be true? My soil is rich with gold and cobalt, my forests breathe life into the world, and my rivers flow with power. Yet, I am told I must beg for aid. Why? Because every time I rise, you find a way to pull me down. You've left me broken, yes, but not defeated."

She pauses, her voice softening with grief. "Do you know what it's like to lose your children? To see them labor in your fields, only for the fruit of their work to be stolen? To watch them die in wars fought for someone else's power? I carry every scar, every loss, and yet, I endure."

Humor Amid the Fury

Even in her pain, Africa's wit shines through.

- "You call me a developing continent. I call you a developed thief."
- "They say I am the future. Funny, because they've been stealing my past for centuries."
- "You promised me freedom but handed me leaders with Swiss bank accounts."
- "You love my diamonds but hate my people. Strange priorities, don't you think?"

A Call for Justice

Her tone changes, rising with determination. "I do not seek revenge. I seek justice. I do not want pity. I want respect. My resources are not your birthright, and my people are not pawns in your games. I am not your charity case, your colony, or your market. I am Africa—ancient, powerful, and unbreakable."

She looks to the future, her voice brimming with hope. "I will no longer wait for you to save me. My salvation lies within my people. My children are inventors, dreamers, and builders. We will reclaim our wealth, rewrite our history, and define our destiny. And when we rise, the world will finally see me—not as the bleeding woman, but as the greatest woman I have always been."

Key Historical References

- **The Slave Trade:** Over 12 million Africans forcibly taken to the Americas, their descendants still grappling with the legacy of that horror.
- **The Berlin Conference (1884-85):** The arbitrary division of Africa by European powers, sowing the seeds of modern conflicts.
- **Colonial Atrocities:** King Leopold's reign of terror in the Congo, the Herero and Namaqua genocide in Namibia, and apartheid in South Africa.
- **Neocolonial Exploitation:** The role of international institutions like the IMF and World Bank in perpetuating economic dependency.
- **Modern Exploitation:** The environmental and social costs of oil extraction in Nigeria, cobalt mining in Congo, and land grabs across the continent.

The Chapter Ends with a Vision of Hope

As the bleeding woman finishes speaking, the world is silent. Her voice has shaken the halls of power, and her words linger like a thunderstorm.

"I am Africa," she declares. "You have taken so much from me, but you will not take my future. That belongs to me and my children. And when we rise, we will not rise alone. We will rise together, united, unyielding, and unstoppable."

11

The Woman Who Rises

For centuries, she waited in silence, bound by chains, contracts, and the crushing weight of betrayal. She was the continent whose treasures built empires, whose people tilled foreign lands, and whose history was rewritten by those who sought to erase her dignity.

But now, the woman who once bled begins to rise. Slowly but surely, she stitches her wounds and reclaims her agency. She is no longer a victim waiting for salvation—she is a force, a queen, a continent reborn.

The Turning Point: A Woman Reclaiming Herself

Her voice is calm yet powerful. "For centuries, I waited for someone to save me, but now I see—I was always the hero I was waiting for. My strength is in my people, my soil, and my soul. They can't take that from me anymore."

Her children, scattered across the globe by the waves of history—first by slave ships, then by colonization, and finally by economic necessity—begin to return. They bring knowledge, skills, and hope, blending ancient traditions with modern innovation.

"They called it brain drain," she says with a sly smile. "I call it brain gain."

The African Renaissance: A New Dawn

The African Renaissance is more than a vision—it's a movement. Across the continent, countries are redefining themselves, reclaiming their stories, and challenging the world's expectations.

The African Union (AU):

- Founded in 2001, the AU represents a bold step toward unity and self-reliance. Its initiatives range from conflict resolution to economic development, embodying the ideals of Pan-Africanism.
- **Agenda 2063:** The AU's long-term strategy envisions a prosperous and integrated Africa, where the continent's vast resources are used to benefit its people rather than outsiders.

Pan-African Unity Reimagined:

- Leaders like Kwame Nkrumah and Julius Nyerere dreamed of a united Africa, and while those dreams were deferred, they were never extinguished. Today, Pan-Africanism is finding new expression in cultural, political, and economic collaborations.
- The **African Continental Free Trade Area (AfCFTA)**, launched in 2021, is a key example. By creating a single market for goods and services across 54 countries, AfCFTA aims to reduce dependency on external powers and foster intra-African trade.

Rwanda: A Model of Resilience

Rwanda's story is one of unimaginable pain followed by remarkable recovery. After the 1994 genocide, which claimed nearly a million lives, Rwanda chose not to remain defined by its scars but to rebuild.

- **Governance:** Under President Paul Kagame, Rwanda has prioritized unity, stability, and development. While Kagame's leadership is not without criticism, his government's focus on efficiency and accountability has made

Rwanda a beacon of progress.

- **Technological Innovation:** Rwanda has embraced technology as a cornerstone of its development.
    - The country launched **drone delivery services** for medical supplies, a groundbreaking initiative that reduces delivery times to remote areas.
    - Kigali, Rwanda's capital, has positioned itself as a hub for African startups and tech conferences.
- **Environmental Leadership:** Rwanda's ban on plastic bags in 2008 set a precedent for environmental conservation across the continent. Kigali is now celebrated as one of Africa's cleanest cities.

Nigeria: The Tech Giant of Africa

Nigeria, often referred to as "Africa's tech capital," is transforming into a global hub for innovation.

- **Fintech Revolution:** Startups like **Flutterwave** and **Paystack** have revolutionized financial services, attracting billions in investment and creating solutions that serve millions across Africa.
- **Entertainment Powerhouse:** Nigeria's Nollywood film industry is the second-largest in the world, producing thousands of films annually. Meanwhile, Afrobeats artists like Burna Boy, Wizkid, and Tiwa Savage have brought African music to the global stage, winning Grammys and dominating international charts.

Botswana: Turning Diamonds into Development

Botswana is a rare example of a country that has used its natural resources to uplift its people.

- **Economic Stability:** Unlike many resource-rich countries, Botswana avoided the "resource curse" by investing diamond revenues in education, healthcare, and infrastructure.

- **Political Stability:** Botswana's commitment to good governance and democracy has made it one of Africa's most stable nations.

The African Diaspora: A Global Force

Africa's children, long scattered across the globe, are reconnecting with their roots and contributing to the continent's resurgence.

- **Remittances:** The African diaspora sends billions of dollars annually to their home countries, funding education, healthcare, and small businesses. In 2020 alone, remittances to Africa totaled over $40 billion.
- **Cultural Renaissance:** The diaspora is amplifying African voices and culture worldwide.
    - Films like *Black Panther* have celebrated African heritage, inspiring pride across the diaspora.
    - Artists like Chimamanda Ngozi Adichie and Ta-Nehisi Coates are reshaping global narratives about Africa and its diaspora.
- **The Year of Return:** In 2019, Ghana launched the **Year of Return** campaign, inviting the African diaspora to reconnect with their ancestral homeland. The initiative drew thousands of visitors and generated millions in tourism revenue.

Achievements Across the Continent

Africa's resurgence is not confined to one country or sector—it is a collective effort.

- **Ethiopia's Green Energy Revolution:**
    - Ethiopia is investing heavily in renewable energy, with projects like the **Grand Ethiopian Renaissance Dam** poised to make it a leader in hydropower.
- **South Africa's Scientific Milestones:**
    - South Africa is leading the way in scientific research, hosting the **Square Kilometre Array (SKA)**, the world's largest radio

telescope project.

- **Ghana's Political Leadership:**
    - Ghana continues to set an example with peaceful democratic transitions and a growing focus on good governance.

Humor Amid Triumph

Even as she rises, Africa hasn't lost her sharp wit.

- "She learned to say no. Now, when suitors come, they leave their wallets at the door."
- "She told them, 'If you want my diamonds, you'll pay the bride price first.'"
- "They called it aid. She called it reparations without interest."
- "They said, 'You're the future.' She replied, 'Funny, I've been the past, too.'"

The Queen Emerges

The bleeding woman is no longer bleeding. She stands tall, adorned not in stolen jewels but in the pride of her people. She is no longer waiting for suitors because she knows her worth.

"I am not just Africa," she declares. "I am the beating heart of the world, the cradle of humanity, and the hope of the future. They tried to break me, but I am unbreakable. They tried to silence me, but now I roar."

The Chapter Ends with a Vision of Unity

She envisions an Africa where her children don't dig in mines but build the technologies that power the world. An Africa where her diamonds fund schools, not wars. An Africa where her voice is as powerful as her resources.

"They called me the bleeding woman," she says, her eyes gleaming. "Now, they will call me queen."

She stands at the edge of her land, her face bathed in the golden light of the setting sun. The winds carry whispers of her past, but the air is filled with the sounds of renewal—builders hammering, children laughing, and leaders debating the future. She is no longer the bleeding woman, no longer the victim of her suitors. She is Africa—the greatest woman—and today, she reclaims her crown.

Her Scars, Her Strength

Her scars are deep, etched into her soil, her rivers, and her people. But they no longer weigh her down; they are symbols of her survival.

- **The Chains of Slavery:** "You tore my children from my arms," she says, her voice heavy with sorrow but unbroken. "You shackled them, sold them, erased their names. But my children endured. They sang songs of freedom, carried my spirit across oceans, and now, they are coming home—not just in body, but in spirit."
- **The Lines of Division:** "You divided me at Berlin, slicing through my tribes and families as though I was a map to conquer. But look now—those borders you drew? My children are crossing them, building bridges where you built walls."
- **The Exploitation of Resources:** "You took my gold, my diamonds, my oil. You polluted my rivers and scarred my land. But I've reclaimed it. Now, my diamonds build schools, my oil powers my cities, and my forests breathe life into the world."

Each scar is a chapter of her story—a reminder of her pain but also of her resilience. They do not define her, but they tell the world: *I have endured, and I will rise.*

A New Chapter: Building Herself Anew

Africa's resurgence is no accident. It is the result of determination, unity, and the refusal to remain silent.

The Return of Her Children: Her diaspora, scattered across the globe, has become her greatest strength. They return not just physically but emotionally and intellectually, bringing back skills, ideas, and investments.

- **Innovators in Lagos:** Nigeria's tech scene is booming, with entrepreneurs creating solutions for finance, healthcare, and education. Startups like **Flutterwave** and **Andela** are putting Africa on the global tech map.
- **Farmers in Accra:** In Ghana, young returnees are modernizing agriculture, using technology to boost yields and reduce dependency on imports.
- **Teachers in Kigali:** In Rwanda, educators from the diaspora are shaping a new generation, blending global perspectives with local knowledge.

Economic Independence:

- The **African Continental Free Trade Area (AfCFTA)** is a game-changer. By reducing trade barriers and fostering regional collaboration, Africa is becoming less reliant on external powers.
- Nations are renegotiating unfair contracts. In Tanzania, late President John Magufuli demanded better terms from foreign mining companies, ensuring more wealth stayed in the country.
- **Local Value Addition:** Instead of exporting raw materials, African nations are focusing on processing and manufacturing locally. From cocoa in Ivory Coast to cobalt in the DRC, Africa is determined to reap the full benefits of its resources.

Unity in Diversity:

- The African Union is stronger than ever, with initiatives like **Agenda 2063** driving a vision of prosperity and peace.
- Regional blocs, like ECOWAS and the East African Community, are fostering closer ties, proving that Africa's diversity is a strength, not a weakness.

Her Crown: Built by Her People

Africa's crown is not adorned with stolen jewels—it is crafted from the spirit of her people, the richness of her cultures, and the beauty of her lands.

- **Her People:** From the bustling markets of Addis Ababa to the tech hubs of Nairobi, her people are thriving. They are no longer defined by stereotypes of poverty but by their innovation and resilience.
- **Her Culture:**
    - Afrobeats dominates global playlists, with artists like Burna Boy and Wizkid headlining international festivals.
    - Nollywood, once dismissed, is now a billion-dollar industry, telling Africa's stories to the world.
    - African fashion, from Ghanaian kente to South African beadwork, graces runways in Paris and New York.
- **Her Land:**
    - Africa's natural resources are no longer extracted for pennies. Nations like Botswana and Namibia are leading the way in ensuring that diamonds, oil, and minerals benefit local communities.
    - Her forests, rivers, and savannas are protected, with initiatives like the **Great Green Wall** combating desertification and climate change.

The Closing Message: A Challenge to the World

Her voice rings out, steady and powerful.

"I am the greatest woman—not because of what they took from me, but because of what I've built despite it all. You called me weak, yet I endured. You called me poor, yet I am rich in ways you cannot measure. You called me broken, yet I am whole.

"I am not your victim. I am not your charity case. I am your equal. And now, I am your challenge."

She pauses, her gaze sweeping across the horizon. "You saw me as a land to conquer, but now you will see me as a force to respect. My children no longer beg for seats at your table—they are building their own."

A Vision of Unity

Her vision is clear: an Africa that stands as one, united in purpose and pride.

- **Her children work together:** Borders no longer divide her. Her nations trade with one another, share knowledge, and support each other's growth.
- **Her voice is heard:** Whether it's on climate change, global trade, or peacebuilding, Africa's voice is respected on the world stage.
- **Her future is hers:** The wealth of her lands stays within her borders, fueling schools, hospitals, and dreams.

Her Message to the Reader

To the reader, she extends a challenge: *How will you see me now?*

- Will you see me as the land of poverty or as the land of promise?
- Will you see my people as victims or as innovators?
- Will you see my scars as marks of defeat or as proof of my resilience?

"I am Africa," she says, her voice filled with pride. "I am the past, the present, and the future. They called me the bleeding woman. Now, they will call me queen."

Her Future, Her Crown

Africa stands tall, her crown shining not with stolen gold but with the radiance of hope and determination. The world watches, humbled and inspired, as she takes her rightful place—not at the margins, but at the center of the global story.

Her scars glisten in the sun, her voice echoes across the world, and her children walk beside her, building a future that is truly her own.

She is Africa. She is the greatest woman. And her story is far from over.

Appendix: Documented Evidence of Western Exploitation of Africa

This appendix compiles a broad range of historical and contemporary evidence illustrating how Western powers have exploited Africa. From the brutality of the slave trade and colonial resource extraction to the subtle yet pervasive influence of neocolonial economic policies and modern regulatory hurdles, these records underscore the complexity and longevity of external intervention in African affairs.

1. The Transatlantic Slave Trade (16th–19th Centuries)

- **Primary Documents:**
  - *Portuguese Royal Decrees* sanctioning the export of enslaved Africans (16th century) are held in the Portuguese National Archives.
  - *British Slave Trade Abolition Acts* (1807–1833) stored in the UK National Archives.
- **Key Historical Facts:**
  Over 12 million Africans were forcibly transported to the Americas. European powers such as Portugal, Britain, France, Spain, and the Netherlands built massive fortunes on the labor and suffering of enslaved Africans.
- **Scholarly References:**
  - David Eltis, *The Rise of African Slavery in the Americas* (Cambridge University Press, 2000)
  - Eric Williams, *Capitalism and Slavery* (University of North Carolina Press, 1944)

2. The Scramble for Africa and Colonial Rule (Late 19th–Mid 20th Century)

The Berlin Conference (1884–1885):

- **Primary Documents:**
  - Minutes and General Act of the Berlin Conference available in the German Federal Archives.
- **Key Historical Facts:**
  European powers divided Africa among themselves without any African representation, ignoring ethnic and cultural boundaries and sowing the seeds of future conflict.
- **Scholarly References:**
  - Thomas Pakenham, *The Scramble for Africa* (Avon Books, 1991)
  - A. Adu Boahen, *African Perspectives on Colonialism* (Johns Hopkins University Press, 1987)

Colonial Atrocities and Resource Extraction:

- **Congo Free State (Under King Leopold II):**
  - *Casement Report* (1904) detailing human rights abuses, available in British archives.
  - Adam Hochschild, *King Leopold's Ghost* (Houghton Mifflin, 1998) describes the system of forced labor and terror leading to over 10 million deaths.
- **German South-West Africa (Herero and Namaqua Genocide, 1904–1908):**
  - German colonial military directives in the German Federal Archives.
  - Isabel V. Hull, *Absolute Destruction: Military Culture and the Practices of War in Imperial Germany* (Cornell University Press, 2005).

3. Neocolonial Structures and Economic Dependence (Mid–Late 20th Century)

Post-Independence Economic Dependencies:

After independence, many African nations found themselves caught in webs of foreign-controlled financial systems and trade networks.

France's CFA Franc Zone:

- **Primary Documents:**
  - Treaties and monetary agreements in French archives and the Banque de France's historical records.
- **Scholarly References:**
  - Ndongo Samba Sylla, *The CFA Franc: French Monetary Imperialism in Africa* (Pluto Press, 2020)

Structural Adjustment Programs (SAPs) by the IMF and World Bank (1980s–1990s):

- **Primary Documents:**
  - Loan agreements and conditionalities available through the World Bank archives.
  - IMF staff reports and letters of intent from African finance ministries.
- **Effects:**
  SAPs forced African governments to privatize state-owned enterprises, cut social services, and open their markets to foreign goods—often crippling local industries and exacerbating poverty.
- **Scholarly References:**
  - Joseph Stiglitz, *Globalization and Its Discontents* (W.W. Norton, 2002)

  - Howard Stein, *Beyond the World Bank Agenda* (University of Chicago Press, 2008)

4. Corporate Exploitation and Resource Extraction (Late 20th–21st Century)

- **Multinational Corporations and Mining/Oil Deals:**
  - **Primary Documents:**
    - Contracts between African governments and foreign companies (e.g., De Beers, Shell) sourced by investigative NGOs like Global Witness.
  - **Case Studies:**
    - Nigeria's Niger Delta: Shell and other oil majors have profited immensely while oil spills devastated local ecosystems and communities.
    - Democratic Republic of Congo (DRC) and Cobalt: Child labor and unsafe working conditions documented by human rights organizations (e.g., Amnesty International reports).
  - **Scholarly References:**
    - Jedrzej George Frynas, *Oil in Nigeria* (LIT Verlag, 2000)
    - Siddharth Kara, *Cobalt Red: How the Blood of the Congo Powers Our Lives* (St. Martin's Press, 2023)

5. Political Manipulation and Support for Dictatorships

- **Cold War Proxy Wars and Puppet Regimes:**
  - **Primary Documents:**

        - Declassified CIA documents showing involvement in the Congo crisis (Mobutu Sese Seko) available in the U.S. National Archives.
        - French diplomatic cables documenting support for dictators in Francophone Africa.
    - **Examples:**
        - U.S. support for Mobutu Sese Seko, enabling decades of kleptocracy.
        - France's role in propping up regimes under its *Françafrique* policy.
    - **Scholarly References:**
        - Susan Williams, *White Malice: The CIA and the Neocolonialization of Africa* (PublicAffairs, 2021)
        - Frederick Cooper, *Africa Since 1940* (Cambridge University Press, 2002)

6. Contemporary Regulatory Barriers and Financial Burdens (21st Century)

In the modern era, exploitation is not solely limited to resource extraction or direct intervention. Western nations have developed systems of financial and bureaucratic barriers that disproportionately affect African citizens.

Exorbitant Visa Fees and Restrictive Travel Policies:

African travelers seeking to visit the European Union, the United States, or the UK face increasingly high visa fees, stringent requirements, and extensive documentation. These policies hinder educational exchanges, business trips, family reunions, and medical travel, effectively curtailing African mobility while generating revenue for Western governments.

Impact on African Mobility:

These visa fees and regulations act as a modern tool of economic extraction, forcing African applicants to pay substantial amounts with no guarantee of success. Frequent rejections and non-refundable fees compound the financial burden, often amounting to hundreds of millions of dollars collectively over time.

Data Sources for Visa Fees:

- Official government websites (e.g., U.S. Department of State, European Commission for Schengen Visas, UK Home Office).
- Reports by advocacy groups and think tanks examining global migration (e.g., Migrant Rights Network, African Union Commission on Migration).

Table: Approximate Increases in Average Tourist Visa Application Fees for Africans (2000–2020)

Year	U.S. Tourist Visa (B1/B2)	Schengen Short-Stay Visa (EU)	UK Standard Visitor Visa	Notes
2000	~$100	~€35	~£36	Baseline fees; limited digital processing
2005	~$131	~€60	~£50	Adjusted as security checks & admin costs rose
2010	~$140	~€60	~£68	Schengen held steady, UK increased for currency changes
2015	~$160	~€60	~£83	U.S. increases for added security; UK increments
2020	~$160	~€80	~£95	Schengen raised fees to €80 in 2020; UK fees continue to climb

Note:

- These figures are approximate and represent the standard tourist visa fees. They do not include additional costs such as biometric fees, appointment fees, travel to consulates, courier services, or the opportunity cost of time and repeated applications.
- The increases outpace inflation in many cases and are significant relative to the average income in many African countries, making travel disproportionately expensive. For example, as of 2020, the $160 U.S. visa fee could represent a substantial portion of an average monthly salary in some African nations.

Conclusion

From the early horrors of the slave trade and the brutality of colonial conquest to the subtle chains of debt, structural adjustments, and modern non-tariff barriers like visa fees, Africa has faced centuries of external constraints on its sovereignty and mobility.

The documents, treaties, policies, and data presented here provide a factual basis for understanding these complex legacies. Whether through direct resource extraction, political manipulation, or regulatory burdens that hamper mobility, these practices have contributed to Africa's ongoing struggle for equitable treatment, genuine self-determination, and global respect.

Acknowledging and studying this documented evidence is an essential step toward recognizing the resilience of African nations and their capacity to shape their own destinies. It challenges readers to understand Africa not through a lens of victimhood but as a continent forging its own path, pushing back against unjust systems, and rising toward a future defined by its own values and ambitions.

Don't miss out!

Visit the website below and you can sign up to receive emails whenever Kayumba David publishes a new book. There's no charge and no obligation.

https://books2read.com/r/B-A-KRSOC-JMGKF

Did you love *The Greatest Woman: Every Man's Desire*? Then you should read *Cry Africa The Western Guide on How Not to Fail the Continent*[1] by Kayumba David!

[2]

In the annals of international relations and global politics, there exists a well-worn play-book: a set of strategies and tactics honed over decades, if not centuries, designed to maintain control, extract resources, and perpetuate power.

This book, "How to Fail a Continent: The Western Guide to Supporting Dictators and Looting Resources in Africa," is a satirical exposé of that play-book, illuminating the dark realities of exploitation and manipulation that have left an indelible mark on the African continent.

1. https://books2read.com/u/bzyGoG

2. https://books2read.com/u/bzyGoG

My name is Kay David, and I have spent years studying the intricate and often nefarious mechanisms of global power dynamics. As an author and observer, I have seen first-hand the devastating impacts of these strategies on the lives of millions.

This book is not just a critique but a call to awareness—a challenge to the status-quo and an invitation to reflect on the real-world consequences of policies and practices that prioritize profit over people.

In writing this book, my aim is to strip away the veneer of benevolence that often accompanies Western interventions in Africa. Through rich sarcasm and biting wit, I hope to lay bare the hypocrisy and moral bankruptcy of systems that, while professing to bring development and democracy, have often brought only suffering and strife. Each chapter dissects a component of the playbook, from the selection of puppet dictators to the orchestration of crises, revealing the underlying motives and machinations at play.

It is my hope that readers will engage with this material not only as a satirical critique but as a serious commentary on the urgent need for more just and equitable international relations. The time for change is now, and awareness is the first step toward action.

I dedicate this book to the countless individuals who have suffered under the weight of these exploitative practices and to those who continue to fight for justice and equity in global affairs. May their voices be heard and their struggles recognized.

Thank you for taking the time to read this book. I encourage you to reflect on its messages and consider how each of us can contribute to a more equitable and just world.

Read more at www.zcews.org.

About the Author

Kayumba David is an accomplished author known for his works that span across themes of spirituality, African experiences, and healthcare chaplaincy. His writings often delve into profound social, political, and personal subjects.

One of his notable works is "Visas: The Irony of Freedom", where he critiques the paradoxes faced by many Africans regarding international travel and freedom

He also authored "Hope and Healing: A Chaplain's Handbook," which reflects on his experiences as a chaplain and emphasizes the importance of compassion and spiritual care in healthcare and prison environments

Kayumba's works reflect his personal journey through theological study and lay ministry, having faced challenges within religious institutions, especially during his time in Belgium, where he became an advocate for open theological debate

His contributions in literature offer insights into African realities, the complexities of modern spirituality, and the role of chaplaincy in emotional healing.

Read more at www.zcews.org.

www.ingramcontent.com/pod-product-compliance
Lightning Source LLC
LaVergne TN
LVHW090043160826
845672LV00013B/628